A Generous Lover is the true and very queer tale of one soul's journey through the wasteland of mental illness to deliver their lost love.

Brimming with psychedelic proletarian prose and trenchant wit, it recounts the pandemonium of navigating mental health services on behalf of a loved one whilst being transfeminine – and occasionally mistaken for a patient.

Drawing on epic poetry, classical mythology, and queer modernist literature, *A Generous Lover* fuses psychology, euphonic prose and song, to create an intimate and beguiling world.

A GENEROUS LOVER

La JohnJoseph

A GENEROUS LOVER

OBERON BOOKS
LONDON

WWW.OBERONBOOKS.COM

First published in 2019 by Oberon Books Ltd
521 Caledonian Road, London N7 9RH
Tel: +44 (0) 20 7607 3637 / Fax: +44 (0) 20 7607 3629
e-mail: info@oberonbooks.com
www.oberonbooks.com

PB ISBN: 9781786829894
E ISBN: 9781786829887

Cover photography © Attila Kenyeres (*A Generous Lover*)
Anna Mimouni (*Boy in a Dress*)

Cover typeface © Fredrik Andersson (FreddeLanka) (*A Generous Lover*)

eBook conversion by Lapiz Digital Services, India.

La JohnJoseph is a British-born, American-educated artist and writer, they have written four ensemble pieces, five solo plays, and one libretto. They have presented performances at the Royal Opera House, Deutsche Oper, Bristol Old Vic, Barbican, Art Basel Hong Kong, Schaubühne, SF MoMA, Dixon Place, Martin-Gropius Bau, Fancy Him (Tokyo), La Java, and Museu de Arte Contemporânea de Niterói. La JJ has also contributed to catalogues, zines, and anthologies internationally for over a decade. Their first foray into prose fiction, *Everything Must Go* (ITNA) was shortlisted for the Polari First Book Prize and a LAMBDA Literary Award.

@LaJohnJoseph (Twitter)   **@la.johnjoseph** (Facebook)

Notes on the plays

These texts were written (and re-written) between 2008-2018, during which time they were almost constantly revised, both onstage and on the page. Through a decade of rehearsal and performance, I found them to be quite literally, different every night. As such, there is no definitive version of the texts, but I hope this publication captures some of their essential (if nebulous) form. The songs mentioned in the scripts are a cornerstone of the performances, but are impossibly expensive to license in a publication like this. With that in mind we've made a playlist where you can hear them. You can scan the QR code or follow the link at the beginning of each play, and see how they inform the script.

This volume was made possible thanks to Arts Council England's Developing Your Creative Practice fund, and Hawkwood College, who provided me with the residency time in which to edit the texts. Further thanks is extended to my friends and collaborators over the past ten years, especially Anna, Jordan, Helen, Sarah, ASJ, Stevie, Sophie, Max, Jack, Erin, Jeffrey, Tucker, and

Andrew, to George Spender for picking me up, and Serena at Oberon for delivering the goods, and of course to my very own Mr Boopie.

Here's hoping you get something out of these two plays, maybe even a candlelit performance in your kitchenette some snowy night when the leccy's out, who knows? And if after countless minutes of trying, you still can't find anything of worth on these pages, don't blame me, blame Chris Brett Bailey.

With fondest wishes, your friend,

La JJ

A Generous Lover was first performed at Summerhall (Edinburgh), and was developed with support from the Wellcome Trust, Arts Council England, Camden People's Theatre, the BAC, Vogue Fabrics, and The Glory. It was directed by Alexandra Spencer Jones, with musical direction from Helen Noir. The cover image was shot in Berlin by Attila Kenyeres, with make-up by Sarah Hartgens, both of whom have graciously allowed use of the picture.

Playlist

https://spoti.fi/32ODr78

Written in three voices but performed as a solo work. The text is set in a continuous soundscape of found sound, atmospheric original compositions, and snatches of almost recognisable pop radio hits. The voices are;

LA JJ:

The author's natural voice, the play follows their experience.

JOAN:

The voice working class Liverpudlian woman, she is direct but she is wise.

PERSEPHONE:

The voice of a mid-century movie queen. Heightened, gracious but intimidating, she is the cod-classical narrator.

Onstage there is a white folding medical screen, a white wooden lawn chair and a free-standing white Corinthian column. The set sits inside a salt circle, which is not quite closed. On the lawn chair we see a purse, a pair of sunglasses and a pair of gloves. Atop of the column is a working tape deck which is used as a practical prop throughout, it plays both original atmospheric soundscapes and the more familiar musical interludes.

LA JJ enters, cautiously moving to close the salt circle. They then approach the column. After a pause of hesitation, they press play on the tape deck, and an instrumental of 'Do You Know The Way To San Jose?' plays. LA JJ sings along for a while, then breaks off to speak.

LA JJ: I wrote this in a psychiatric institute, scribbling away in the little red notebook I'd bought for our trip to Kyoto. I wrote this in prison, scrawling furtively, hoping that the big boss wouldn't catch me in the act, and impound my little red notebook. I wrote this surrounded by the dead and the undead, lost souls and celebrities, in a place teeming with mythical creatures, great artists, and mobsters. I went there, to that place, to Ospedale, all for the love of a man, Orpheus. And I've come back from that shattered, shabby hell to tell of this tale of devotion, demonic possession, and the dissolution of the line between stardom and insanity.

PERSEPHONE: Welcome, beloved. We stand ready to embark on an adventure into a territory for which there is no map, no official record, only this tale to recount that which our dearest Orpheus endured. From here on in, you may rest assured that everything described, every impossible triumph and humiliation, is true. How do we know? Well, beloved, because we were there to witness it.

JOAN: Yeah, I saw the 'ole thing with me own eyes, I swear down. So yous can take this as gospel.

'Do You Know The Way To San Jose?' reprises with a big band version of the music coming through the house speakers. LA JJ sings the second half of the song, then returns to the story at hand.

LA JJ: Well, it came out of the blue. After a few nights of broken sleep, and a few days of steadily increasing activity, Orpheus told me, "I'm going to call Dionne Warwick and ask her to sing this song I just wrote."

I politely asked, "Do you mean the Dionne Warwick? 'Walk On By' Dionne Warwick?" He simply glared and replied, "Yes JJ. The Dionne Warwick, it's for my film, it's going to win the Oscars."

Orpheus had always been a little eccentric let's say, but that's why I loved him, because he functioned according to his own rules. We had been in love for almost seven years, and there had never been a dull moment. He had recently enrolled in an MA film making course, and was already thinking BIG.

I tip-toed on, "I don't really think Dionne Warwick sings theme songs for student films anymore."

He lost his cool, he said, "JJ you don't get it – you're not on the same level as me, my work is amazing, you don't understand! I'm not manic, I'm just realising that all my dreams are coming true and we're going to get the millions and the beach house in LA, and I'm going to teach you how to drive. Yala! Look JJ I'm serious! I love myself! I've learned to love myself."

LA JJ moves to the lawn chair and sits in it, despondently.

I realised that some miles back the road had forked, and we'd taken the wrong turning. I recognise now, that I should have grappled with the steering wheel before we went over the edge, but hey, that's the beauty of hindsight.

Orpheus continued, "Come on, my tutors think my film is amazing. They asked to see fifteen minutes of my film, but I've done is so incredible, I've already sent them eleven hours because it's one of the most incredible films ever made and I'm not even joking."

He showed me the film, or rather part of it, because in his heightened state he couldn't sit still for more than a few minutes. Wide-eyed, he entered into a wild dialogue with the film, shouting back and forth at the screen. Then he insisted on googling pet insurance, then he took off all his clothes to take polaroids of himself naked. And they say men can't multi-task.

I didn't understand what was happening, I asked him if he was high.

He barked, "No JJ! I am not on drugs, you know I am not allowed to take drugs because of my condition! You're stressed JJ. So breathe! Deeply, from the diaphragm! I'm going to practise for my concert now, I'm making an album JJ. I'm sorry but it's my turn to be a star now!"

So I sat there in my bewilderment, breathing deeply from the diaphragm thinking, "What the holy fuck is going on?"

To soothe me Orpheus strummed on his guitar, playing 'What's Going On?' by The 4 Non-Blondes, over and over, and over, only changing the lyrics autobiographically, to better describe the great successes and sorrows of his own life. It was a thick melodic stew of medieval troubadouring and white girl with dreads slam poetry. I did not know what was going on but I had an inkling.

I was afraid, I was confused, but wasn't I just a little bit amused? Charmed even. To see this impish spirit take over Orpheus, he who had all too often drowned in deep pits of depression. Listening to him jam joyously, I wondered if madness isn't always a little seductive?

LA JJ sings 'The Man With The Child In His Eyes'.

PERSEPHONE: *(Rising from the chair and
striding to the column, clutching the purse.)*
Orpheus is confused, Orpheus is talking
in double time, incoherent, aggressive,
grandiose, exaggerated, picking fights with
strangers, and then sobbing as he remembers
his mother's death. Orpheus is buying drones,
and iPhones as presents, spending much
more money than he has, his big brown
eyes supersized by the dark circles engraved
beneath them. Orpheus is singing out loud,
in the streets, and yelling *(this phrase is heard
as a recording on playback)* "Entschuldigung!
Tut mir leid! Verzeihung!" Three different
ways to apologise in German.

Orpheus is scaring his friends, with
heightened, garbled phone calls which
come in the middle of the night, oscillating
between effusions of love, and vague threats

of a forthcoming reckoning. Orpheus is descending into the underworld again, and no one, no man, no demi-God, no TV personality, can reach him, can persuade him to turn back.

Orpheus cannot see us, he doesn't hear us begging. We've implored him to remain with us, to stay away from Pluto's Gate, not to trespass, but Orpheus will not listen. He's insistent.

Engulfed in a long cloud of smoke coming from his vape pen, he turns to regard us over his shoulder and then vanishes from sight with these final words *(again this phrase is heard as a recording on playback)* "Don't follow me!"

PERSEPHONE produces a vape pen from the purse and exhales a cloud of smoke through her nose.

LA JJ: A few days of ragged, mumbled, delusions followed. Orpheus took to wearing an old lady's grey wig, and talking in riddles. He hardly slept, he would lay awake talking elaborate nonsense until almost dawn, at which time he would have decided that the contents of the bedroom needed to go into the living room, and the contents of the living room needed to go into the garden, and no-one could argue with him. Our roommate moved out, the dog took to hiding under the table, and I found every possible excuse to stay out of his way. I was hardly surprised then when his film professor called me from hospital and asked that I come straight away.

When I arrived Orpheus was docile, peaceful, almost content. He was drawing with coloured pencils in a notebook and listening to Billie Holiday on his headphones. I loved him. I don't think he knew why we were there. His professor dispelled my sense of tranquillity when he said, "I'm sorry. But I have an obligation."

Eventually we saw a doctor who said, "Orpheus, we think you need some help. We think you are experiencing a manic episode. Do you understand what that means?"

"Yes!" Orpehus shouted, "But what I don't understand is why you are telling me this. And anyway who are you? Are you even a doctor because you look like a child. What are you Doctor Dougie Howzer? I am getting out of here and I will sue you because Theresa May is right! The NHS needs to be closed down."

This was the first time on this adventure, but not sadly the last, in which I was made aware just how fine the line is between being clinically insane, and being a Conservative.

The doctor tried to get things back on track, "Now Orpheus, that's not the issue at hand here."

"No!" Orpheus said, "The issue at hand here is that JJ gave me AIDS!"

For a moment I became the red-faced centre of attention, as I tried my best to form a cohesive sentence in my own defence. I could barely splutter, "I, I, didn't! Honestly, I didn't."

Orpheus yelled, "I want an HIV test right away, and if I don't have AIDS you're going to send me home, right Dougie? Right?"

Like some angel of peace the doctor nodded, "Yes Orpheus, we can of course get you an HIV test."

Orpheus smiled at the doctor, glared at me, "Good, thank you, so do your job."

"But," the doctor continued, looking to his colleagues for consensus, "I'm afraid, we can't let you go home."

PERSEPHONE: Beloved Orpheus was familiar with the underworld, perhaps you have heard the tale? Anyone would think that such a sad story would bar him from ever returning. But, Orpheus is no longer in control. He is compelled to return to where he is forbidden, bowling headlong into that verboten territory, reckless of the risk. Aware of his trespass a council is assembled, one doctor, one senior doctor, one social worker.

PERSEPHONE: Orpheus, you are unwell

LA JJ: Orpheus, I think you need help.

JOAN: Orpheus, will you accept treatment?

Orpheus replied discourteously *(this phrase is heard as a recording on playback)* "Never! I refuse! Entschuldigung!"

PERSEPHONE: And so it is decided, "Section 2". That as he was unfit for the land of the living, Orpheus would be condemned to the underworld for all eternity.

LA JJ: Well, twenty-eight days to be extended at the doctor's discretion.

LA JJ sings 'Leave Behind', during which they pick up a pair of gloves from the lawn chair and put them on. They then unfold the medical screen, revealing a Sacred Heart motif. At the end of the song, they return to the story.

LA JJ: Mania is heads to the tails of depression, on the great giant bastard coin of bipolar disorder. If depression is a fellow characterised by the inability to even climb out of bed, then mania is his horrible symbiotic twin. Mania makes the sufferer feel untouchable, erodes all of their boundaries, making them capable of doing anything and saying anything, at any time. Truly mania is a generous lover who makes you feel so good about yourself that you never want her to leave. From the outside that might sound quite a wonderful state to be in, who wouldn't want to be invincible? And while I have the opportunity to say it, yes, having sex with someone who is experiencing a manic episode is quite frankly, fantastic. But, it's accompanied by a darkened chaos of reckless behaviour, re-mortgaging the house, and spending hundreds of pounds on handmade wigs for auditions on *Britain's Got Talent*.

The night they took Orpheus to Ospedale, he was quaking, he was afraid, he clung to my arm, whispering, "Don't leave me JJ, don't leave me here."

One of the other patients barrelled up to us and declared, "I'm Gerry Adams! I'll blow yous all to kingdom come! Up the IRA!"

Well, I was quite shocked! Gerry Adams? What a throw back reference! I mean, I know the nineties are back, but still.

Orpheus begged the nurses so that I could stay with him, as though I was his mother and this was his first night away at summer camp. And it was heartbreaking, horrifying, having to abandon him there, afraid and sedated. I went home and cried my guts out, tossing and turning unable to sleep, anxiously waiting for the gates to open again the following day.

JOAN: You new 'ere? I haven't seen you around 'ere before 'ave I? That your mate over there with the 'eadphones on an' the leccy ciggy in 'is gob? He looks alright really. Sort of. My name's Joan. My al' fellas in 'ere an' all. Dead 'andy like 'cos I only live on the estate across the road, so I can pop in an' see 'im whenever I need to. Not that he knows I'm here like. He's away with the fairies, full time that one.

I says to 'im, I says, "You alright there, you daft al' bastard? 'ave you had your breakfast?" Doesn't say nothin', never does.

But I tell you what la, every time I nip out for a cig an' a Lucozade I thank me fucking lucky stars that I'm not banged up in here meself! I'd go barmy!

Oh, but, there's some real characters in 'ere I'll tell ya. See 'im over there? Tried to kill

'imself with a broken bottle didn't 'e? That's
why 'is 'arms are all bandaged up like tha'.
All 'is fingers are bound together in them
dressings, so he looks a bit like a great big
crab. I call 'im the Lobster King 'cos he walks
around like 'e rules the fuckin' place.

And that's Les, that's actually 'is real name,
doesn't suit 'im though does it? He just
doesn't look like a Les. To me, 'e seems more
like a Eugene. Anyways 'es the one always
asking you for a cup of water, so's 'e can pour
it on the floor, an' make puddles to splash
about in, the poor bastard.

An' see 'im, the er, black lad? Oh 'e's gorgeous
isn't 'e? An' dead sweet an' all, 'e's been 'ere for
six months already, an' you never 'ardly 'ear a
peep out of 'im. Except when 'e's apologising
for somethin' 'e 'asn't even done. I call 'im
The Wounded Saint. We always think 'e's

20

goin' 'ome, but thee always bring him back again. Honest, 'e's in and out of this place more often than my sheets are in an' out me washer-dryer. Well, it's just a very sad place isn't it? But you do get used to it, eventually. An' you can ask me if there's anythin' you need, I'm always 'ere like.

The melody from 'Somewhere Over The Rainbow' is heard from off stage.

Oh 'ere we go, Judy's off again, thought she'd been quiet for a while! See 'im? The al' fella with the 'at on? I call 'im Judy 'cos 'es always singing "Somewhere Over The Rainbow". Well I say singing, it's more caterwauling really isn't it? Not that I'm the kind of person to be rude about other people's disabilities. But sometimes you do wish they'd be a bit more generous with the sedatives.

Oh, and ook at 'im, the little one. Breaks my heart 'e does! Always talkin' to 'imslef like. He can't be more than twenty-three, where's 'is Mother? You know, 'e's the only one who never asks about gettin' out, I think 'e knows 'e's in for the long haul. Always shufflin' bout in 'is slippers, like one of the little princes in the tower. He's Spanish like, so I always call him El Infante. Oh but it's a shame though? Makes you wonder if there really is a God.

PERSEPHONE: *(Puts on the sunglasses and lounges in the lawn chair. She makes a dramatic gesture for the music coming over the speakers to be cut before she begins to talk.)* So Orpheus languishes in Ospedale the kingdom of the undone, populated by every sort of misfit outcast psychopath, fighting amongst themselves like dogs. And who walks with him? Refugees from the land of the living,

complicated, fearful, scurrying, medicated
men, men deemed by the limits of the law,
likely to cause harm to themselves or others.
Hear the groans of men wandering aimlessly,
the elderly singing songs from the movies,
the terrified teenagers who don't know why
they're here, the belligerent lifers.

>*PERSEPHONE journeys to the tape deck and
>presses stop/eject. The soundscape halts.*

LA JJ: I was as a neon infringement in
Ospedale being neither a male inmate, nor a
female visitor, as was the traditional divide.
I somehow blurred the lines, a suspicious
hanger on, by refusing to declare myself
on either side of any border, with my
transdrogynous self-presentation.

I was always so very aware that even in living
memory, people like us could have been

condemned to a place like this, for no other reason besides the tender connection that united us. So I was very suspicious of the doctors and of the vision of normality they upheld as proof of cure. More so I was aware that I made the staff uncomfortable.

LA JJ flips the tape in the deck and presses play, a cacophonous soundscape of chatter is heard.

When I reflect on that place now I'm glad I kept such thorough notes, or else I might easily convince myself it was all but a nightmare.

When Dante took his own trip into the Inferno, he declared, "I called all of my conscious to note each facet of this rotten hole and also of the persons burning here." This was not Hell, but it was lit by a similar fraternal infernal illumination. I brought

Orpheus as many pillows and blankets as
I could carry but I knew what bleak little
comfort these reminders of the world outside
would offer.

The whole place had an awful, medicinal,
urinal, smell to it. To call the place
Dickensian would be too high of a
compliment, really it was little better than
borstal. It was always dirty, and the nursing
staff were never any kinder than they had to
be. I could see that they were afraid and worn
out themselves. They huddled in their Perspex
box occasionally looking up from their
phones, and staring out at the rabble that
surrounded them, weighing up how necessary
it was to talk to any of them.

The doctors were even more unapproachable,
they would sweep through the ward once
or twice a day like medieval Bishops, with

the whole populaces surging towards them
for blessings, for exorcisms, and they would
push past with as much contempt, into a
hermetically sealed chamber, keeping out of
sight as much as possible.

The general atmosphere then, was part
monastery, yes, prison yes, but also part chem
sex party. You see, patients were strictly kept
from any "intimate contact with romantic
partners", which meant there was always
an uncomfortable air of sexual frustration,
a predatory behaviour stalking the floor.
Orpheus told me that the Lobster King had
shown him his dick and asked if he liked it.
Maybe not unusual behaviour in one of the
Berlin night clubs where our own love affair
was born, but certainly it was unsettling in a
mental health ward.

Orpheus said, "He wants to fuck me JJ, and he's the boss. I don't want to get on the wrong side of him. He runs things in here."

The Lobster King was pretty intimidating, heavy set, tall, with his hands bandaged up like claws. Sidling up to me, but gesturing to Orpheus he said, "Eh! I like your friend."

I did my best to ignore him. I just carried on reading a discarded copy of the *Daily Mirror*, so he put his claw on my shoulder and said, "Oh yeah, reading are ya?"

"Yes," I said, "I'm studying for Holy Orders."

Sensing all the intended disrespect in my manner, he wrapped his bandaged fist tight around a packet of Benson and Hedges, crushing the whole contraband pack of fags.

"Your cigarettes!" I pointed, wondering if he was aware of what he had done.

"Don't matter," he snarled. "I ain't got a lighter anyway. Had to sell it to some geezer in here didn't I?"

In the meantime, Orpheus had ordered a pizza from Deliveroo, it arrived now but was not to his liking.

"JJ," he said, "I can't eat this! You know I can't eat anything spicy because of my hernia. I haven't done anything JJ, you know that. So, call my lawyer, call my family JJ, and get me out!"

And he ran to the window, pounding on the plastic panes with his fists, yelling "GET ME OUT!"

This elicited little response from the staff, busy as they were sharing Lol Cat videos.

The other inmates all took it in their stride too. Besides Les, for whom Orpheus' attempt at escape must've sparked memories of old Saturday morning superheroes, because he started to chant, *"Na-na-na-na-Na-na-na-Na BATMAN!"*

Now, the one nicknamed Judy took a pointed dislike to this, because it was interrupting re-runs of *The X-Factor*, and Lord knows Judy loved his sing-a-longs. Swivelling himself around on the pleather sofa, he shouted to Les, *"Ah! Fuck off you wanker!"*

Les' tart retort proved he was occasionally aware of his surroundings, because he replied, "No, you fuck off, you old bastard!" And the whole thing descended into quite a fracas. Well, enough to prompt a nurse to come out of the ivory watchtower and ask, "What's this all about then?"

Entirely upstaged, Orpheus regarded the scrum with an aloof shaking of his head. Woefully he said, "JJ, I'm just going to give this pizza to some of the crazy people." And he hopped about offering slices of holy pepperoni to the deserving. I thought that was really very generous.

PERSEPHONE: Take a look around beloved, at the plight of these lost souls. The Wounded Saint begging forgiveness for imagined misdemeanours, and El Infante looking more afraid and reclusive everyday. His lover, Novia, comes to visit, but when he looks at her, he looks through her, and she looks almost as worn through as he.

As though he were a child again, in short pants again, the Lobster King tries to catch the attention of a nurse, who perhaps simply over capacity chooses to ignore him. He calls after her, "Miss?" "Miss?", but his plea has no effect. So he sinks back into the sofa, back into the stupor, back into the solitude of the dispossessed. The meek shall inherit the Earth, we know, but when?

LA JJ sings 'All Delighted People', coming to kneel in front of the Sacred Heart screen at the conclusion of the song.

LA JJ: Even in ugly places there is beauty, maybe ironic beauty, maybe sentimental beauty, but still. Because beauty and ugliness hold hands, they are sisters, one always contains the other, or so Bataille claimed. But in Ospedale, there was not a trace, and that is what made it truly abysmal. Everything was bathed in a yellowish light, which made the place seem weightless and nauseating. The bathrooms had no toilet seats, no taps, and only plexiglass mirrors, as if no expense

had been spared in sanding away anything
decorative, anything comforting, as a thief
files the serial number from a stolen bike.

Due to security concerns, only plastic cutlery
was permitted, no glass was allowed, and all
electronic cables had to be stored with staff,
in case someone tried to hang themselves,
with a MacBook Pro charger. All of these
prohibitions, this list of deadly household
items, made the place feel even more
dangerous. Which of course it was. Because
in amongst the mix of the gently senile,
the massively neurotic, and the endearingly
demented, there were bona fide killers. One
unlocked door led to a patient absconding, not
to be returned to custody for over two weeks,
in which time he'd stabbed someone to death.

The terrifying, dissociative uniformity of the
ward created an atmosphere of ambivalent

horror. The patients sat about listlessly, hunched in corners, talking to themselves, threatening each other under their breath. It was like a scene from a Hogarth etching, grown men lying shirtless, twisted and confused on any surface that suggested some comfort.

And always the staff, at pains to tell me, "We aren't bad people, we don't want to hurt anyone. And we certainly don't want to keep anyone here any longer than we have to." I found myself nodding to this, as if hearing their confession. But now, from outside of the hospital, I shudder a little. I wonder now if the nurses weren't making the kinds of disclosures Proust tells us that murderers, and broken hearted lovers alike, are compelled to admit.

I arrived at the hospital one afternoon, late for the start of visiting hours, and found Orpheus balled up on a couch sobbing, alone. His eyes were swollen with fear and bewilderment. He said, "They're drugging me JJ. They hold me down to inject me."

JOAN: *(Perching on the arm of the lawn chair.)* I don't know how they expect anyone to get better in 'ere, I really don't. For a start, the food is absolutely diabolical. It's the worst grub I've seen in me 'ole life, and I grew up on a council estate in Bootle! They've got these jaundiced sandwiches, which look like somebody's been at the edges with a curling tong, to get the perfect Farrah Fawcet flip on the crusts, and these measly, slimy salads on paper plates. I mean, nobody wants to eat tha la'! Nobody!

JOAN takes off her gloves.

Of course, no one's allowed near the kitchen neither, are thee? No. The nurses are terrified, that Judy Garland and Gerry Adams might get together and make an explosive device from the microwave and a family pack of pot noodles. So the 'ole place is always strewn with chippy wrappers, night and day. It's absolutely filthy – looks like dirty al' Tracey Emin's been through doin' one of 'er artworks, the mucky cow.

An' I mean, just look at that thing on the wall. The what d'you call it? Oh aye, yeah, the *muriel* on the wall there. That is so bad it's actually offensive, I am actually offended by actual the sight of tha'. An' it's clearly the work of a professional; you can see the resentment in every brush stroke. You've got these two clouds painted in the middle, an' they're grinnin' at each other like a right pair. I think that's supposed to be a rainbow above them, but to me, it looks more like a stream of psychedelic piss. I mean how is this good for anyone's mental health? An' do not get me started on that that tatty al' banner! Friggin' 'ell. It says, "Don't let a stumble be the end of your journey." But I tell you wha', every time I see that I all I can think is, "I'm sorry la but if you're in 'ere, looking at this it probably is the end of your fuckin' journey."

JOAN vapes and exhales smoke from her mouth contemplatively.

LA JJ: *(Rises from the chair and walks to the column.)* Off from the side of the formal dining room, the ward also offered an art therapy salon, where the cooler, sexier kids sat about vaping and playing music to each other from their phones. It was not at all unlike Berghain at six a.m. on a Sunday morning. The conversational was very chill, everyone was so strung out on antipsychotics and tranquillisers. That's the thing about the mentally ill, they are very good listeners, and are not at all judgemental.

The walls of the art therapy room were a looping patchwork of bold bon mots, pages from colouring books which had been illuminated by the patients in felt tip and crayon. They read "Don't stop believing!" and "It's always darkest before the dawn" and "What if I can?"

I always found that one particularly troubling, "What if I can?" I wondered, "Is it wise to suggest this to people in these various psychotic states, *What if I can?*"

"What if I can escape out of the window? What if I can persuade Katie Price to marry me? What if I *can?*"

For those who grew bored of colouring in *All You Need is Love* posters, there was almost an entire library, stocked with such classics as, *The Tarantula Keeper's Guide*, and *Best Baby Names 2010*, and, my personal favourite, *Guns'n'Ganja: the Bob Marley story*.

Now, Orpheus was becoming increasingly frustrated by this extended confinement, and by the company he was forced to keep. He'd had enough of the Wounded Saint, he was through with El Infante, he was sick of the Lobster King. To make things worse, the doctors had forbidden him to take out a bank loan so he couldn't even buy a farm in California. He was very upset. I foolishly laid my arm around his shoulders, but he was only more agitated by my tactile attempts to soothe him.

Flinging my arm away he hollered, "Look JJ, I'm sorry but I'm not gay. I have just been experimenting with gay sex!" And, never one to miss an opportunity for high drama, he darted out of the room, leaving everyone staring at me as I turned a shocking pink and just rage-doodled.

I spent a lot of time in the art therapy salon, because it was the calmest place to be, calm being of course a relative quality. The place was usually a cacophony of YouTube prank videos layered over a choice cut from the hospital DVD library, usually something uplifting, like *Girls Aloud Live at Wembley*.

I was becoming acclimatised to the place, like a befuddled visitor to the Magic Mountain, the five to eight hours a day I spent there seemed meaningless compared to the unknown weeks and possibly months of visiting hours, laid out before me in the mists of time.

I once sank so so deep into thought in there, that I didn't notice when everyone else shuffled off to the bathroom, or to take their medication. It took me sometime to recognise, that I was in fact sitting there, chewing a felt tip pen, and watching the "making of" feature on the DVD of *American Pie 2* – entirely alone.

LA JJ, PERSEPHONE, and JOAN sing 'Candidate', trading the lyrics quickly between them throughout.

JOAN: *(Standing irate at the column.)* You know, the thing that really gets to you, the thing that really gets on my fuckin' wick, is how they treat them like there's no 'ope for them. I wanna say to them nurses sometimes, "You don't have to talk to 'im like that you, condescending cunt," but I don't though, because I've already 'ad a talking-to from the doctors for me language, an' I don't want another, not so close to Christmas.

I reckon, if I 'ad a couple a quid, like 'alf a million or somethin', I'd take our Frank out of 'ere and put 'im in somewhere decent. 'Cos you know they don't stick you in a place like this unless you're poor an' you can't do no better. Oh aye, I know. I went an' saw a private psychiatrist with our Frank over in the West End didn't I? Cost us six 'undred quid just for the consultation it did!

Now, when you go private do you think they treat you like this? Do thee shite! You get your own room with an en suite, you get to pick what you want for your dinner, no one manhandles you, an' get this, right, they even give you *bottled water!* No, I'm not kiddin'! I took two, one for the bus ride home like.

The doctor says that Frank'd have the best quality of treatment of course, but if he was gonna stay there, in the private hospital with the lovely net curtains and a CD player in every room, it was gonna be almost a grand *per night!* I said, "You wha'? That's more than EuroDisney costs for the week!" They're robbin' bastards aren't thee?

An' the doctor says, "Mrs McDermott, I do understand the costs may seem steep. Some of our patients decide at this juncture to sell their houses, in order to cover the costs of care."

Well I just laughed, an' I said, "Oh aye, sell the 'ouse? Can't imagine the council will be very pleased with that la!"

So that was that an' here we are. But I tell you what, I took all them magazines off the waiting room table home with me din't I? The robbin' bastards.

LA JJ: *(Sits in the lawn chair.)* The pharmacist
came to sit next to me, whilst I was writing
out these very notes. She said, "Orpheus, I
want to talk to you about your medication."
She was only slightly embarrassed when I
explained, "I'm actually not a patient here.
Orpheus is over there, trying to sellotape
a vape pen into a sketch book." But I
shuddered a little at how easy it was to make
that mistake.

I had been there so long, watching the other
patients coming and going, and they didn't
seem *so* unusual anymore. I started wondering
if I had been admitted myself, and if not *why*
not? Freud says we fear what we most desire,
it's the return of the repressed. Maybe then
this is what I most desired? To be buried alive
here, next to Orpheus in Ospedale.

After a month of steady begging on his part,

and assurances of keen vigilance on mine,

I was allowed to escort Orpheus outside to

smoke. The Lobster King and the Wounded

Saint had already earned this privilege, so I

accompanied the three of them into the car

park. *(LA JJ wheels the screen downstage so it*

becomes a wall.) The outside world had never

looked so unappealing.

Instinctively they snook around the side of the

building, trying to avoid the sight of whatever

authority they thought they were under.

We stood around a pile of old newspapers,

the *Metro* I think, with the Prime Minister's

grimace glaring up at us from the front page

like the head of the Medusa. The three smoking

gorgons looked down at her sorrowful, as they

took puffed on their cigarettes. Moved by an

unknown impulse, the Wounded Saint knelt

to pick up a copy of the paper, and sudden moment of realisation washed over the face of the Lobster King. He said to me, "Eh! Ain't I seen you in the papers?"

I shook my head, "No, not me, you must be thinking of someone else."

Orpheus interjected "JJ is always in the papers, JJ is a very famous singer."

"Really, I'm not," I said and waved away this, what was it? This accusation, this daydream, this projection.

The Wounded Saint had meanwhile opened up the paper and found a picture. He said with glee, "Look! That's you innit? In the papers!"

It wasn't.

"No," I said. "That's Eddie Redmayne."

But, the Lobster king tutted, unconvinced, "Nah, I know I've seen you in the papers."

Orpheus continued, "Come on! JJ is always in the papers, don't listen! JJ is always in the papers!" He was clinging to the Lobster King's arm like some sycophantic courtier, driving him deeper into this delusion and sparking another bout of frantic page flipping on behalf of the Wounded Saint who found a new page and exclaimed, "Look! That one's you innit? In the papers!"

I was impatient, but I was flattered. I said, "No, that's Tilda Swinton. Honestly, I am not in the *Metro*!"

"Not today," hissed Orpheus, "But you always are! And if you don't stop lying about everything you will never, see me ever again!"

And right on cue, having found another picture on another page, the Wounded Saint practically exploded with glee, waving the paper above his head, saying, "Look! That's you! That is you innit? In the papers!"

The Lobster King guffawed, "I knew it, I knew it!", and I finally lost my cool.

"Look," I said, "*That* is quite clearly a picture of Margaret fucking Thatcher. I am not in the *Metro*! So give me the bastard paper and stop going on about it!"

I snatched the paper from his hands, and threw it on the ground just as it started to rain. I felt quite guilty about that, but stopping to pick it up would have ruined the gesture.

In all seriousness, Orpheus said, "Oh my God! Do you see what I have to put up with? JJ is such a diva."

JOAN: Where were you this morning then la? Well you missed out I'm tellin' you that much. You know how they had to cancel the table tennis class 'cos Judy and Gerry kept battering each other with the racquets? Well guess what they've booked instead? No, I'll tell ya. They've booked a Zumba instructor. I'm not kiddin'.

So she comes in 'ere, Carol or whatever she's called, unzips 'er fleece and plonks her boombox down right in front of the telly, an' she's all, "Come on everybody, now it's time to Zumba!" But the only one the nurses can persuade to join in is Les, but he's so far gone 'e doesn't know where 'e is 'alf the time. He just stands there pullin' faces and pointin' his

fingers above 'is 'ead like 'es doin' the Sat'day
Nigh Fever, only without so much of the
pelvic thrustin' thank God. But Carol's goin'
'ell for leather isn't she? "Come on everybody,
now it's time to Zumba!"

But everyone else is just snorin' away on the
couches, except for al Les who's at it down the
front doin' the Monster Mash like. Oh my
God, it was a sight! I tell you wha' though,
she was at it for the full sixty-minutes, gotta
give it to her for professionalism. I thought
your friend might've joined in because 'e
always seems very, erm, energetic but 'e said 'e
'ad a film to finish. Well I thought he meant
he wanted to watch the end of *Ghostbusters* or
something, but no, 'e meant that 'es actually
makin' a film. And he's asked me if I'd like
to participate! I said I'd be happy to star in
his picture, but that I draw the line at any

profanity, an' I'm not doin' no nude love scenes neither. Well, nothin' below the waist.

LA JJ: Orpheus was sinking too deep into his *Citizen Kane* fantasy to even realise when I was there. He only noticed me when I'd gone. He'd call me all through the night when he couldn't sleep asking for things he needed. I spent all my time away from Ospedale baking banana bread, and figuring out how to smuggle in Xanax, and phone chargers. Eventually I brought in cigarettes too, because the Lobster King had taught Orpheus how to disable the smoke alarm in the bathrooms. "It's fine JJ," he said, "It's what everyone does in here." I was his girl on the outside you see. I was like Holly Golightly sneaking secrets to Sally Tomato in jail, only I knew what I was doing.

Orpheus had very few other visitors, a trip to Ospedale wasn't exactly at the top of anyone's list of priorities. A friend of his aunt came by with a handbag full of condoms for him. "He asked me to bring them," she said, scanning the room with barely concealed horror. "But what does he want them for in here though?" That was her only visit.

Our friend Helena came by too, but one afternoon of being being draped in Turkish Airline blankets and forced to wear the grey old lady wig and was all about as much as she could endure.

You see, Orpheus could erupt apropos of nothing with incessant cruelties. Madness makes you so inventive with your invectives. He said to me, "JJ you're a failure. You have failed at everything in life, and that's why you keep clinging to me! Because you see me being *so successful,* and you want to take it all away from me. Well no more JJ! The problem is that I am from a professional Jewish family and you are just a working class Catholic. I'm sorry JJ but you're from the wrong social class for me."

If you're wondering why I didn't just leave in the face of such sharpened unkindness, you have to understand that I grew up knee-deep in poverty, violence, and chaos. I'm basically Tonya Harding with slightly better wardrobe, and a much worse sense of humour. So, none of this was new to me. But it was enough to rouse a nurse from her primordial slumber to say, "Orpheus seems to be particularly distressed today. So I'm going to have to ask you to leave now JJ. You can come back tomorrow, if he wants you to."

"I don't!" he yelled.

So I was escorted out, thinking to myself, "Well! You've just been thrown out of a mental hospital. That's a new low isn't it?"

And it just sort of went on like this for a few weeks, a few months. I kept on hoping that the medication and the counselling, and maybe even the Zumba, would have a beneficial effect. I kept praying that I'd get him back, that the real Orpheus would return to me. But the longer we lingered, the more I began to panic; "What if this was the real him?"

Then there were times of almost sweetness, which somehow hurt more. Like the time he made me a cup of herbal tea with barely warm water and said, "JJ, I'm sorry, I love you, I want this to be over. Let's go away somewhere."

And it was as though my prayers to God, to the doctors, to anyone who listened, had been heard. It was like the storm had passed. But the mania always returned, and the clouds always rolled back in. It was like that brief, beautiful moment three minutes into, Whitney Houston's 'I Will Always Love You', when you think she's finally stopped singing. But no, she comes back with ever greater passion, to belt out another fifteen choruses and you say, "We are not out of the woods yet."

Before I could even reply, Orpheus had slipped off, saying, "Shh! JJ. I have to help Les now! Les needs me." Les was sitting shirtless in a pool of water, moaning to himself. He was unaware of Orpheus who fluttered about him, massaging his shoulders and repeating, "I'm so proud of you baby, so proud."

LA JJ sings 'Waiting', folding the screen up to its original position during the song.

LA JJ: I couldn't see any discernible improvement, but the doctors claimed to. Orpheus wanted to be released into the care of the friend of his aunt who'd brought in the handbag full of condoms, but the doctors insisted that they needed evidence that whoever agreed to take him home was capable of such a grave responsibility. Our friend Helena politely declined, there was it seemed, only me. I thought it was too soon. I didn't think that I had the capacity to make sure he took his medicine every day, or to ensure he was in bed by ten p.m. each evening. I thought I'd barely be able to get him back home before something horrible happened again. But I could see how desperate he was to be free, so I gave in.

I told the doctors what they wanted to hear,
Orpheus nodded along with all of their terms
and conditions, not meaning to abide by any
of it, and they let him leave. *(LA JJ presses stop/
eject on the tape deck a final time.)* We put
all of his stuff in black bin bags, and piled
it in the doorway as we waited to be let out
one last time. A small crowd had gathered,
Orpheus didn't want to talk to any of them,
and I felt ashamed of this final coarseness. El
Infante stared at us, the Lobster King hustled
for a fag, and the Wounded Saint said, "Oh.
Is your friend going? I'll miss him, he plays
nice songs on the guitar."

As soon as we got home, Orpheus booked
himself a flight to Los Angeles. I thought
about calling the hospital, I thought about
betraying him, but he would've hated me. And
I would have hated myself for sending him

back there. So I stepped aside, and let him
pack his suitcase. I had failed Orpheus and I
had no more fight left in me. I tore a page out
of my notebook, and wrote him a letter, to tell
him how much I loved him, and I slipped it in
his suitcase. Then I slipped a sleeping pill, and
went to lie down in our old roommate's bed,
so I wouldn't have to watch him leave. I think
I heard him talking to the dog, andI think I
heard the wardrobe doors opening and closing,
all through the night, but when I woke up in
the morning, he was gone.

PERSEPHONE: And so, here ends the tale
of our beloved Orpheus, free now from that
oubliette where his troubled mind had led
him. Free to walk, to run, to fly. They say
he made it all the way to San Jose, that he
bleached his hair platinum blond, and hired
a convertible to drive along the coast. From

time to time news reaches us here, none of which can be verified now, because Orpheus has crossed the line from fantasy to folklore.

JOAN: It's not gonna be the same in 'ere without you love. It's been dead nice 'avin' you 'ere. You take care of yourself alright?

LA JJ: I think of Katherine Hepburn. Well I *often* think about Katherine Hepburn, but in particular, I think of her in *The Lion in Winter*. She plays Eleanor of Aquitaine, a sort of medieval super-villain. *(LA JJ moves to the lawn chair and sits down.)* There's a scene where, realising that she has failed to secure her freedom, she breaks down before her dressing table mirror. She says, "I've lost again. I'm done for this time! What a desolation." *(LA JJ gathers the glasses, gloves and vape from the chair and puts them in the purse.)* But then, remarkably, she pulls herself up, she adjusts her crown, and declares, "Oh well, there'll be other Christmases."

I think of that Katherine Hepburn/Eleanor of Aquitaine hybrid, like the two-faced God Janus, looking backwards and forwards out over time simultaneously, and that's where I find peace. When I think of Orpheus and I madly in love, on the ferris wheel in Blackpool, both terrified, clinging to each other, certain that the creaky old monstrosity would surely come apart, and deposit us into the inky black night sea. Or when I think about that afternoon on the beach in Athens, when the water was still warm enough to swim even though it was November, and the two of us fucked in the midweek, midday sun. Or when I think about our trip to Kyoto, and how we cycled through the freezing cold mid-March nights, drunk, and singing Simon and Garfunkel all the way.

When it seems too hard to put one foot in front of the other, when it seems I can't take another day of this bastard world, I remember Blackpool, the beach, and the bike, and I know that I haven't entirely wasted this gift of life, whatever it is meant to be. Because once I loved someone, and he loved me. You see I have had Paradise, so I have Paradise, and I keep it always with me. *(LA JJ takes out the tape from the deck and puts it in the purse.)* And yes Eleanor, yes Katharine, *"There'll be other Christmases."*

*The climax of 'I Will Always Love You' plays loudly and **LA JJ** lip-synchs sincerely for a few seconds, before breaking character.*

LA JJ: *(Gestures for the music to be cut.)* I'm just kidding.

Fin

Printed in the USA
CPSIA information can be obtained
at www.ICGtesting.com
LVHW020840171024
794056LV00002B/306

9 781786 829894

Boy in a Dress follows the life story of La JohnJoseph: a Trans*, fallen Catholic, ex-fashion model from the wrong side of the tracks.

In this autobiogaraphical, raucously political, and accidentally profound piece, La JohnJoseph brings together an outrageous but heartfelt slew of true-life tales of catholicism and drag, public sexuality and body dysmorphia.

BOY IN A DRESS

La JohnJoseph

BOY IN A DRESS

OBERON BOOKS
LONDON

WWW.OBERONBOOKS.COM

Boy in a Dress was first performed at Ovalhouse (London) and was supported by Arts Council England and crowdfunding donations. The original production was directed by Sarah Chew, with musical direction from Jordan Hunt. The part of The Anima was originated by Anna Lewnhaupt, and subsequently played by Erin Hutching, in the Edinburgh production and on tour. The text of *Boy in a Dress* comprises material from three earlier works, which we drew together in rehearsal, to make one "retrospectacle". These works were *Notorious Beauty* (directed by Tucker Culbertson and first presented at Dixon Place, New York), *I Happen To Like New York* (first presented at Bistrotheque, London) and *Underclass Hero* (directed by Jeffrey Gordon Baker and first presented at the Royal Vauxhall Tavern, London). The cover image was shot in Berlin by Anna Mimouni, with the permission of whom we use it here.

Playlist

https://spoti.fi/2YhFOMd

Written for three performers, with a good degree of fluidity between them as to who plays which role when. These voices are;

JOHNJOSEPH:

The central character from whom the other two personae emerge. They are a world wandering storyteller and this is their autobiography.

THE ANIMA:

The female alter-ego, the physical realisation of the narrative, she conducts her explorations through frantic personae switches.

THE PIANIST:

The male alter-ego, the musical expression of the narrative, an accompanist and a confidant.

All three characters wear red knee high socks and gold glitter platform shoes as their base, on top of which they continually build new looks and identities from the costume draped about the stage. The stage is never empty, the play is a continual cat and mouse game, between the three characters.

*We are in a space that is transient; boxes, storage, interesting bits of rubbish, waste paper, a broken mirror and a disco ball. At the centre of the stage, amidst the detritus, stands a large, battered wardrobe. A soundscape plays, it is made up of the sounds of the sea, FM radio, church bells, and the noise of the fairgrounds, Coney Island and Blackpool Pleasure Beach. **THE PIANIST** is visible, sitting on a box, half dressed.*

*As the house lights go down, **THE PIANIST** starts to explore the space, with a flashlight. He puts on his gold shoes, and a tailcoat, busies himself moving boxes. When he reaches the piano, he plays a few chords as if testing it out. Amongst plastic sheeting on top of the wardrobe, **JOHNJOSEPH** is revealed, in an orange cocktail dress. They begin to talk, apparently continuing an ongoing conversation.*

JOHNJOSEPH: And did I tell you? Entirely of my own free will, I attended a lecture on Foucault recently. The boy sitting next to me

raised his hand to quiz the professor on his apparent intimacy with the great thinker. He said: "Excuse me, Professor, but did you ever even meet Foucault?'

The professor replied: "Meet him? My dear, he shat in my mouth."

Foucault says that we know what we are because we know what we are not, the Other is our necessary twin. If you have spent your entire life imagining the world to be fabricated from building blocks with repellant charges, that hold the universe upright through the strength of their opposition, if you know yourself to be a man because you are the inverse of a woman; if you have built your entire lifestyle, eating habits, choice of soda, DVD collection and selection of white button down shirts on this sacred principle,

equivocation may feel like global collapse on
a hamburger bun to you.

*JOHNJOSEPH climbs down from the wardrobe
on a ladder.*

I was helpless, homeless, and hopeless.
I had a university degree worth less than the
paper it was printed on, which had bagged
me a job selling perfume at Penhaligons, to
the decrepit and despotic of the financial
district. I constantly prayed that bejewelled
finger of fortune would single me out for
a life less ordinary, but Fortune seemed to
be busy elsewhere, and so I returned each
evening, Cinderella style, to sleep on the
sofas of begrudging pals, and back each
morning to the oppressive tedium of the
fragrance counter.

My one sustaining grace in life was that in my boredom I had figured out how to access Myspace via the till point. So it was without the slightest consideration, forethought, deliberation or planning, I accepted as soon as it arrived in my inbox, a most unusual offer. Inexplicably a dear friend of mine, Gina, had found herself managing a hotel in New York. Her offer was as straightforward as it was random; that we marry, run the hotel together, and that I relocate permanently to the big apple.

Upon receiving this invitation I turned to my co-worker, lovely girl, mouth like a sailor, and I said "Darlinda look, I have to split. Quite simply, I have realised, that this is not my place of magic. To be frank with you, gift wrapping bottles of toilet water is just not my bag!"

I continued, "Do I or do I not have a first class degree in philosophy from Oxford?"

"No," she replied, "You have a 2.1 from King's in American studies."

I said, "Darlinda, you are right, you are absolutely right! I am out of here – and by here I mean this country. I have been here more than twenty years and it is quite clear I have outstayed my welcome!"

And with barely more than a suitcase full of old dresses and a family photo album, I was off. *(**JOHNJOSEPH** shines the torch into the theatre aisle.)* Diving head first into the golden sunshine of the American dream. I woke up in Brooklyn, in two foot of snow. You see, there was just one thing I had overlooked, just one factor, I had not taken fully into consideration – reality.

*JOHNJOSEPH slowly turns and, as they do so, the mirrorball is activated and **THE PIANIST** plays 'The Apple Stretching', **JOHNJOSEPH** sings.*

*As the song ends, **THE PIANIST** continues to vamp the music. **JOHNJOSEPH** disappears behind the wardrobe, then reappears, drops a pair of schoolboy shorts, and exits the stage again. **THE ANIMA** enters from wardrobe, dressed identically to **JOHNJOSEPH**, picks up the schoolboy shorts herself and exits again through the wardrobe. **JOHNJOSEPH** re-enters immediately, having changed from the cocktail dress into a schoolboy's uniform.*

JOHNJOSEPH: In May 1982 Pope John-Paul II made a visit to England. He was the first ever Pope to do so, and called for peace in Northern Ireland and an end to the Falkland's war.

The crowds that met him in the London were relatively modest; 3,000 at Westminster Cathedral, 4,000 at Southwark, but as His Holiness traveled further north they swelled. 350,000 in Coventry, 200,000 in Manchester, and when he arrived in Liverpool, a crowd of one million people came out to greet him, a great ocean of devotion swelling up from that deeply devout, desperate city, filling the streets and the services he presided over. As the sunset that revelatory day in Liverpool, a day in which all conversation centred on this visit from the Holy Father, my nineteen-year-old Mother went into labor. I was born in the last few hours of the papal visit, and so my deeply superstitious and personably spiritual Mother named me JohnJoseph, in honour of the pontiff and my grandfather.

Clocks and watches, cats and dogs, knives
and forks and spoons, when I was a child
everything was gendered to me.

"A cat is a girl and a dog is a boy, and they get
married."

> *THE ANIMA appears from the wardrobe also
> dressed as a schoolboy.*

THE ANIMA: No it's not. *(She throws one
of her gold shoes onstage.)* A cat is a cat,
it's a different species. Different specieses
don't even get married. *(She throws a book
downstage.)*

JOHNJOSEPH: "The fork is the lady and the
knife is the man."

THE ANIMA: But what about the spoon? *(She
throws a set of spoons.)*

JOHNJOSEPH: *(Picks up a spoon.)* He's in the middle.

THE ANIMA sits on wardrobe steps, watching JOHNJOSEPH somewhat mockingly.

JOHNJOSEPH: Of course, now I wear it as a badge of honour that no one ever knows if I am a boy or a girl. It takes the pressure off me from having to decide decisively for myself. But it was very different when I was twelve.

When I was twelve, I was trying to return a pair of shorts at Woolworths, they were too big for me. Being raised a boy, being raised the eldest son, being raised to believe that men are the smarter, stronger, superior sex when I was first referred to as 'she' it was mortifying. I was mortally wounded, I was slashed open right there in that branch of Woolworths, the same branch of

11

Woolworths I had stolen a crème egg from when I was seven. My Mother ordered her second husband to take me back to the store to return the crème egg and apologise. She hated to have to deal with such menial things herself, as much as she hated to wash dishes.

The store manager told me that he knew I had stolen a crème egg because he counted them every night and there was one missing. I wanted to tell him that I knew the order of all of the books in the Old Testament. I wanted to tell that there was no way he had time to count all of the candy, daily. I wanted to tell him that he was a bogus authority figure, but my Mother's second husband looked so embarrassed I didn't have the heart to. I took it, and I empathised with Saint Genet, the patron saint of thieves, that we should both be so chastised over such trifles. We stole to steal a place in the world.

JOHNJOSEPH steps forward and THE PIANIST hits play on tape recorder, ambient muzak is heard, as though in a shopping mall.

JOHNJOSEPH: Erm, I want to bring these shorts back please. They're too big, my Mum says I must get a full cash refund not store credit. And not gift vouchers. Erm, I have my receipt.

THE PIANIST: *(Switching on his lamp.)* Marge! I need a refund! This little girl wants to bring her shorts back.

JOHNJOSEPH: Erm, I'm a boy, a boy actually. I have my receipt!

THE PIANIST: Oh I am so sorry. *(Laughing hysterically.)* I just got a bit confused. I thought you were a girl. It's because you're so pretty.

THE ANIMA, JOHNJOSEPH and THE PIANIST
lip-synch a short burst of 'Don't Go Breaking My
Heart', then all three then return to their place
as if nothing has happened.

JOHNJOSEPH: The experience in Woolworths was, it must be said, psychologically damaging. I was ashamed to have been mistaken for a girl, I felt degraded.

THE ANIMA exits through the wardrobe bashfully.

JOHNJOSEPH: My Mother fell about laughing when I told her, but I didn't hold it against her. I grew up to learn what I don't think she ever has done; that women aren't the stupider, weaker, inferior sex at all. If anything I do identify more with women now than with men. I can't associate myself with maleness without feeling like a rapist.

THE PIANIST presses play on the tape machine again. 'Teacher's Pet' plays, and JOHNJOSEPH performs a clumsy strip routine until they are naked, a physics book from their schoolbag providing the only coverage. Afterwards, THE PIANIST comes forward to hand JOHNJOSEPH a pair of underwear, holding up his coat tail to protect JOHNJOSEPH's modesty as they put them on. THE PIANIST returns to the piano, JOHNJOSEPH finds a red Adidas tracksuit amongst the boxes and begins to dress.

JOHNJOSEPH: People ask me now rather lasciviously, "Oh but wasn't it terribly degrading to be a stripper? Didn't you feel dirty and objectified, and oooooh, totally exposed?" Well, yes, OBVIOUSLY, but it felt not wildly dissimilar to my day-to-day experiences on the street as a third gendered renegade, trying to take public transport without being sexually harassed, mocked, or photographed for a Japanese street-style blog.

I was the first of eight children born to my manic depressive five-times married Mother. We grew up very poor, very religious, we moved around a lot. We were always on the run from some bailiff or social worker, over an outstanding Argos bill, or a dodgy DSS claim, and so we moved around *a lot*. We lived in tower blocks, on housing estates, and in holiday apartments, with my Mother's endless retinue of sex offender, alcoholic boyfriends. It was a lot like growing up in a circus, or a sex cult, only without the camaraderie, or the hope that you might one day be able to leave.

JOHNJOSEPH picks up a small leather suitcase and a leopard print faux-fur coat.

Each time she got remarried we all changed our surname, called the new fellow "Dad" and act as though he was in fact our real

Father, as though she'd never been married before. It really was perfectly ridiculous. We would turn up on a new housing estate looking like a tawdry version of the Waltons, me and my seven siblings, forced to pretend that we were all spewn forth from the same gloopy mixture of secretions though we didn't even look a like. It was like Orwellian double-speak, unlearning everything, and acknowledging that obviously it was all an out and out lie, but simultaneously that it was the new truth.

THE PIANIST plays the opening chords of 'Sweet Child o' Mine'.

JOHNJOSEPH: My Mother faked herself out far enough as to imagine the neighbours believed the ridiculous scenario she was spinning, though I don't think they ever really did. All the same, she would get horribly

mad if we spoke about previous, shall we say, tenants.

JOHNJOSEPH sings 'Sweet Child o' Mine'.

JOHNJOSEPH: The great irony is, I almost escaped growing up in the gutter, I came this close to being sent away when I was six years old. I remember being on the bus with my Mother, with my sisters and our new step-Father, whom I apparently I hated. What can I say I was a misanthropic six year old, I started early. I don't remember being mean to him but apparently I was.

Exactly, how mean can a six year old actually be anyway? What was I doing? Refusing to make him an Easter card out of egg boxes? Ignoring his offers to share a milky bar? I don't know. But I do remember my Mother telling me; "You've got a new Dad now and if

you can't behave properly, nicely then you're
going to have to go and live with another
family. You're not going to ruin this for me."

JOHNJOSEPH sings *'Sweet Child o' Mine'*
(reprise) while kneeling at the suitcase.

JOHNJOSEPH: I remember being on that
bus and knowing that they were taking
me somewhere from where I wasn't going
to return: The Liverpool Family Services
Office. I remember becoming completely
hysterical, on the bus, so hysterical that
we had to disembark from the bus and
walk the rest of the way, all the way to the
Liverpool Family Services Office. Never
let it be said that causing a scene in public
is counterproductive, sometimes it's the
only way. I was on the verge of being taken
into foster care, being packed off to some
pedophile on the Wirral or worse yet,

a childless born again Christian couple
in Cheshire, so really I had nothing to
lose. I think of that moment now as my
introduction to the dramatic arts, and
somehow it worked. By the time we reached
the Liverpool Family Services Office, my
mother had had a change of heart.

So when our social worker asked "Now
Mrs. Hughes, er, sorry, Mrs Sullivan. Have
you thought anymore about a new situation
for JohnJoseph?" my Mother almost looked
almost embarrassed. She said, "Oh no, he's
been so well behaved lately. We've had none
of that old bad behaviour have we? No, he's
gettin' on much better with everyone these
days, so he's going to stay with us. For now."

JOHNJOSEPH sings 'Sweet Child o' Mine'
*(reprise) moving downstage sweeping the coat
about in anger as it concludes.*

THE ANIMA emerges from the wardrobe immediately at the end of the song, dressed in a red sequin dress which is threadbare, carrying large cards in the manner of a Ring Girl at a wrestling match.

THE ANIMA: And did I tell you? In 1949, in her book, "The Second Sex", Simone DeBeauvoir said, "One is not born a woman, one is made a woman." In 1929, in her novel "Orlando", Virginia Woolf said: "A porpoise in a fishmonger's shop attracted far more attention than a lady who had won a prize!" And in 1999, in her essay of the same title, Britney Spears said: "Oops I did it again."

THE ANIMA hands JOHNJOSEPH a microphone and flips the cards to reveal that they each have a cartoon face, drawn in the manner of the children's game 'Guess Who?'

JOHNJOSEPH: If you were to assemble any surviving pictures of my Mother and her menagerie of husbands, you would be forgiven for thinking she was some sort of Victorian monster hunter, so gruesome were her prizes. She married for love, she married for money, she married because she was pregnant, she married because it seemed like a good idea at the time – inevitably, it wasn't.

The 'Benny Hill' theme blares loudly. ***THE ANIMA*** *walks around the audience with her cards above her head, each one represents a step-father* **JOHNJOSEPH** *talks of. She starts with a showgirl smile and walk, but quickly becomes increasingly tired and desperate.*

JOHNJOSEPH: Husband number one! Her first husband, my Father, was a motorcyclist of whom the only memories I have are disappointing. They married when they were

18, and were divorced after two children, and a few tempestuous, violent years. My Mother tells me she knew it was over when he blackened her eye, broke her left arm and shattered her ribs in an argument over Teletext.

Husband number two! She met him almost immediately after, at Secrets Nite Spot, and unsurprisingly given that illustrious meeting, they were married and divorced within four years, after one child. He got the chop when my Mother found him in the bedroom, with his trousers off, in the company of the six-year old girl from next door.

Husband number three! He worked for the Inland Revenue, and really that would be quite enough to condemn him to at least the sixth circle of Hell, but he managed to out do even that nefarious personality disorder by

ditching my Mother for another woman – her sister! He and my Mother had a son together so if you do the maths, you'll deduce that technically that child is both my half-brother and my step-cousin.

*By now **THE ANIMA** is pretty much falling over.*

Husband number four! Now, he was really something. A liar, a cheater, a gambler, a repressed homosexual, an alcoholic and a womaniser. He'd just been dismissed from the R.A.F in rather dubious circumstances, so obviously my mother married him and had two children with him, practically as soon as she met him. He had a strange habit of getting me blind drunk and telling me dirty stories about his life in the military, how he and his military buddies would get together and masturbate. I don't deny that it turned me on, but we didn't take the relationship

any further. I just didn't think that would be appropriate.

*THE ANIMA finally collapses, wraps herself in the leopard faux fur coat, exhausted. **JOHNJOSEPH** sits on the ladder.*

JOHNJOSEPH: When he left her, my mother was completely incapacitated, she went completely off the rails, she went to bed for six months, a year, who can tell in these situations? She was totally incapable of doing anything besides making histrionic phone calls in the middle of the night, and ordering various handheld vacuum cleaners from the catalogue. I was left, quite literally, holding the baby. I would dress him and change his diapers, and get up with him in the middle of the night, and generally parent him. Well, someone had to.

If that seems odd now, you have to remember that were I grew up it wasn't at all unusual for a twelve year old to have a kid. Really just like all the other teenage mums on the estate.

THE PIANIST plays 'Famous Blue Raincoat'. JOHNJOSEPH sings.

THE ANIMA leaves through the wardrobe with the suitcase, as JOHNJOSEPH sings. As the song concludes, JOHNJOSEPH removes the track suit jacket and ties the pink shirt worn underneath, at the midriff, to make the look more stylish and feminine.

JOHNJOSEPH: Everything you know about New York *is* true. I really did have rats, I really did have roaches, and I really did have a crack head living in the doorway. The hotel Gina ran was actually a youth hostel, and three of our mutual friends had also had

the same sensational idea as me, at the same time as me, of moving to New York, living with her, and *making it*. Making what I don't know, all anyone ever seemed to make was toast, or a mess.

THE ANIMA re-enters through the wardrobe in the orange cocktail dress from the top of the show, now accessorised with sunglasses, and headscarf, and the small leather suitcase.

JOHNJOSEPH: That meant that five of us shared Gina's two rooms, with her two cats and no central heating, on the top floor of a youth hostel in Bed-Stuy, Brooklyn's most infamous neighborhood, loved for its drugs and its gang killings through the '70s, '80s and '90s. Whenever I told someone where I lived they'd say; "Bed-Stuy? Like crack wars, Bed-Stuy." That did little to comfort me.

Gina and I spent a lot of time going to parties, in swimsuits, in the middle of the night, or dressed like Joan and Christina Crawford. Many was the time we'd be hurrying through the snow in platform shoes at midnight, when we'd run right into a whole bunch of boys hanging out on the corner, at midnight, and they'd yell:

THE PIANIST: *(In a New York accent.)* "Hey ladies! Looking good!"

THE ANIMA turns, standing shoulder to shoulder with JOHNJOSEPH gives a look of a rabbit caught in headlights.

JOHNJOSEPH: "Don't say anything," Gina would hiss, "Don't speak and they'll never know." She'd squeeze my arm and say, "Smile! For God's sake smile."

THE ANIMA beams a maniacal smile.

JOHNJOSEPH: And the two of us would run off through the snow beaming like a pair of demented beauty queens, trying to maintain someone else's fantasy, for our own security. We'd arrive at some filthy downtown party and inevitably some glammed up drag queen would say to me *(directing the insult to THE ANIMA)*, "JohnJoseph, what are you wearing? You are not a fabulous drag queen, you are just some boy in a dress."

JOHNJOSEPH finds a stack of papers and begins to write frantically, using the lower half of a shop mannequin as a desktop. THE ANIMA speaks JOHNJOSEPH's thoughts aloud.

THE ANIMA: Words get so boring, they're so unoriginal. I am a soup spoon! I have the curves of a fork and the hard edge of a knife. Meanwhile, gender is the keystone in this society of differentiation, it is the

template for black versus white, poor versus rich, us versus them, and people like me rupture it. Do I seem like a slap in the face then? An insult to everything you hold dear? Am I the return of your repressed desires to know other parts of yourself? The parts that your father beat out of you with his heavy leather belt, the parts that your mother made you carry books around on your head to deny? Am I Das Unheimliche, an unexpected mirror image, a sexual fantasy spoken too soon in the relationship? *(JOHNJOSEPH makes a paper plane from the paper they are writing on.)* I am that figure I admit it, I am that folk devil, that pagan intersex Satan. I am that point on the horizon where pink and blue are lost into the purple haze. *(JOHNJOSEPH throws the plane into the audience.)*

THE ANIMA exits through the wardrobe.
JOHNJOSEPH closes the door behind her, and
THE PIANIST throws a paper planes covered in
text to them.

JOHNJOSEPH: It wasn't all bad, nobody's life
is all bad. Except maybe that poor girl who
got locked in an Austrian sex dungeon by her
father for twenty years. But I bet even she
must have managed a little chuckle on the
side, because life is like that. Happiness bleeds
into even the gloomiest of places.

There was in place during my formative
years, a scheme which allowed poor but
intellectually capable children to attend good
schools, nice schools, private schools, paid for
by the government. I can only imagine this
was some sort of drunken oversight on behalf
of the Conservative party, but as I always say,
"Never look a Tory gift horse in the mouth."

*(To **THE PIANIST**.)* I do always say that, don't I?

THE PIANIST: You do always say that, yes.

JOHNJOSEPH: And so, I sat and passed the entrance exam for St Mary's College, a school founded by The Christian Brothers to educate the children of Liverpool's burgeoning bourgeoisie in the true holy mother faith.

THE PIANIST plays the refrain from 'Ave Maria'.

JOHNJOSEPH: And let me tell you, they were thrilled to have me.

JOHNJOSEPH opens the wardrobe to reveal THE ANIMA as Our Lady of the Sacred Heart.

JOHNJOSEPH: I was aware growing up, that being from a piss poor family, none of whom ever managed to even finish high school,

that I had few career options. The docks
had closed, the mines had closed, and I was
clearly not going to play for Liverpool or
Everton. So, it seemed that I had two choices,
I could either join the army like my Mother's
brother or become a priest, as school advised.
I heard the voice of God and believed that
I would obviously become a sacred vessel, a
priest upon graduation, then Arch Bishop,
then Pope. At an early age I recognised my
vocation for sermonsing.

But I knew that with a Mother married more
times than Elizabeth Taylor and with more
children than Mother Teresa, I was already on
very thin theological ice with my conservative
Catholic high school. I knew that if I didn't
finish every piece of homework on time,
I would be out that door quicker than you
can say Jesus, Mary and Joseph!

THE ANIMA gasps.

JOHNJOSEPH: Which you shouldn't say anyway because it's blasphemous.

THE ANIMA nods.

JOHNJOSEPH: All the other children at St Mary's lived in the suburbs, in houses, they had parents, and they ate vegetables. They were driven to school by mums and dads, on their way to jobs in finance and marketing. I walked in, from Bootle, after taking my sisters to school and my brother to nursery of course. And I was often late, and I was often oddly dressed, and what can I say? Some things never change. And despite all of that Catholic hocus-pocus about loving your neighbour and favouring the poor, these brats were not down with anybody who didn't have a Super Nintendo of their own.

Of course, when everyone back on the estate heard where I was going to school, well, let's just say they were less than proud. Thus I found myself in the deliriously undesirable situation of being tormented all week at school, for being such a piece of trash, and terrorised all weekend on the estate, for being a snob and a suck up. I remember coming home early from school one day (I had slipped out before P.E.) and seeing two of the boys who lived a few doors from me, standing on the corner. I looked at them, thinking, "The little blond one's quite cute." I smiled. They didn't smile back, and just as I walked past they spat in my hair. I pretended not to notice.

That was the first time I ever felt what it was like to be truly hated, not just disliked or ridiculed, but actually hated. My head was all mixed up with feelings of flourishing desire,

and the realisation that people were capable of doing really horrible things at the drop of a hat. It was like Eros and Thanatos sixty-nineing in my subconscious.

I remember running my hand across the back of my head and feeling that cold thick, mucous and slime, bringing my hand before my face, covered in crystalline, liquid cobwebs, glinting in the late afternoon sunlight, unable to escape the comparison with a handful of cum, and thinking, "This is how the world has marked me."

THE PIANIST begins to play 'Lovers' Spit'.

JOHNJOSEPH: I don't think I ever really got the spit out of my hair.

The stage becomes a church aisle leading to the statue of Our Lady in the wardrobe. JOHNJOSEPH sings 'Lovers' Spit'.

JOHNJOSEPH: Catholicism was the major aesthetic and theological influence on my teenage self, I think that's clear. My sister was the May Queen, she got to wear her white communion dress to lead the procession to Church and crown Our Lady with a wreath of flowers. I was so jealous, I couldn't speak to her for a week. I should have been the May Queen! The mystical power of Catholicism got inside me, it was a major source of comfort to me, it was my first psychedelic experience, it gave me the transcendent visual capacity to see the beauty in the filth – not separate from it but in it.

JOHNJOSEPH walks towards the Virgin, kneeling to finish singing 'Lovers' Spit' (reprise).

JOHNJOSEPH: *closes doors on **THE ANIMA** and sits on the steps of the wardrobe.*

JOHNJOSEPH: There was a boy in my class. Isn't there always? He came from a devout Catholic family, he was an altar boy, which meant that by the time he reached his teens he was hell bent on depravity of every sort. His precocious descent into sex and drugs was his own anthemic "Fuck You" to his repressive religious upbringing. I think he chose me, me the best behaved, most impoverished, generally most Tess of the D'Urbervilles-esque side-kick he could find, to enact his Madonna infused scenarios with, just to make them that little bit more salacious.

My new-found schoolfriend invited me to spend lunchtime with him in the school chapel, he said he had something he wanted to show me. I thought to myself; "Oh how fascinating, there must be a detail in one of the stages of the cross I had neglected to

notice! What a most informative lunchtime this will be!" But that wasn't what he wanted to show me, no. What he wanted to show me was how talented he was, how prodigiously gifted he was at oral sex. I admit I was a little surprised the first time he undid my flies, it being the house of the Lord, but then I remembered how often in the Bible Jesus invited his followers to come into His Kingdom, and so I allowed it.

As luck would have it, Mr Hyde, the Religious Education teacher, walked into came into chapel at that most inappropriate moment. The poor fellow must have thought the Book of Revelations was actually coming to pass, right there in his very own chapel. He simply gasped, "Boys! What are you doing?"

Now, you would think, that even with his rather limited understanding of sex, that it

would have been quite obvious what we were doing. But no, he actually asked, "Boys! What are you doing?" And the first thing to come out of my friend's mouth, well, the *second* thing to come out of his mouth, was the word, "Fighting." Yes, "fighting."

And I, caught up in the moment, agreed and said, "Yes, sir, sorry sir, we were fighting sir. Sorry sir."

I've never known if he was simply blinded by the shock of what he saw, or if he had in fact never had a blow job, or for that matter been in a fight, but Mr. Hyde went along with this lame excuse. He took us into his office, and gave us an endless lecture on desecrating the house of God with violence during which all I could think about was the fact that my trousers were in fact full of cum. We were

suspended for a week, when I came back my friend had been moved to another school.

That particular incident sped up our religious education quite dramatically. In my teens being queer inevitably meant that you would contract, and die horribly, of AIDS. It meant not just death in this life, but death in the next, it meant eternal damnation – because *that* was a mortal sin. Once during an especially bleak double period Mr. Hyde instructed us to copy into our notebooks the slogan, "All homosexual acts are deviant and wrong."

*JOHNJOSEPH opens the wardrobe to reveal **THE ANIMA** dressed as a schoolboy again, writing out her lines, "all homosexual acts are deviant and wrong", on a chalk board on the inside of the wardrobe door.*

THE PIANIST plays 'All Apologies' and JOHNJOSEPH sings.

As JOHNJOSEPH sings, THE ANIMA covers the wardrobe and the floor in her lines of chalk. During the song, JOHNJOSEPH begins to erase the chalk lines, causing THE ANIMA to write faster and more frantically. Eventually JOHNJOSEPH takes the chalk from her hand, and replaces it with a UV torch. As the song ends THE ANIMA starts to uncover the UV graffiti, which is scrawled on the floor and on the wardrobe.

JOHNJOSEPH: I started to skip school a lot; some days you just don't want to be humiliated in front of a room full of your peers, you know? I couldn't stay home, my Mother was either shagging very loudly or else embroiled in very physical fights with whomever she was married to slash living

42

with at the time. And so began my love affair with public toilets in the park. Where else was I going to go? I was fourteen, I had no money, it was always raining. I wasn't exactly going to be spending my afternoons at the racecourse, was I ?

JOHNJOSEPH begins to ascend the ladder to the top of the wardrobe.

People say; "Libraries, they're very stimulating places for young people to spend their time, and free too!", which is true, and Lord knows I love a local library, but unfortunately librarians themselves aren't terribly supportive of truancy are they? No, the only people who encourage truancy in teenage boys are drug dealers and pederasts. Thus began my love affair with public toilets, where both types of gentlemen were in steady supply.

THE PIANIST strikes a repetitive note which mimics the sound of a dripping tap. UV lights come on and reveals the whole set to be covered in explicit graffiti, which THE ANIMA explores with glee.

JOHNJOSEPH: I could spend whole afternoons in there, locked in a cubicle. I was absolutely entranced by the graffiti, the puerile and poetic scrawlings of hundreds of lusty, illiterate sexual deviants. Dates and times, obscenities like incantations, vivid, staccato descriptions of previously unimaginable depravities, overwritten, obliterating previous diagrams and hexagrams engraved into the melamine partitions. The most wild fantasies, splashed over every available inch of the wall space, a cacophony of sacrilegious desire, so electrically sexual and suffocatingly perverse, making the place divine, turning each little cubicle into

a confessional, the whole rank lavatorium turned into a church. I loved the graffiti because it was so absolutely, unequivocally, vilely honest. It told of the horrors of desire and the most heartfelt descriptions of the love some anonymous scribbler craved, and honestly hoped to find, in a stinking Liverpool public convenience.

I'm no too sure if any of those queens, those horny old men or those bi-curious passersby, ever did find love, or lasting relationships. But they usually managed to find a pleasant way to pass the time, which is really all anyone can hope for.

THE PIANIST plays 'Man of 1000 Faces'.

JOHNJOSEPH at the top of the wardrobe strips to their underwear as they sing. They descend the ladder at the song's conclusion.

JOHNJOSEPH: However, even I knew that if I ever wanted to do something, be something, that I couldn't spend my whole life dodging social service workers and hanging around public toilets. So I went further afield to find culture and community in Liverpool City Centre.

*With a gloved hand, **THE ANIMA** throws out clothes from the wardrobe, which **JOHNJOSEPH** changes into, deliberately wearing the skirt as a bandeau top, and the t-shirt as a skirt.*

JOHNJOSEPH: By the time I was fifteen I was a regular at the bars and clubs in Liverpool city centre. Somewhere along the way I made friends with a very portly drag queen. She was a DJ, and she became integral to my new-found lifestyle as an underage party girl, because going out with her, no one ever ID'd me, and I didn't ever have to pay.

She would take me in, early, about seven p.m. or so, she liked to use the place as private boudoir, while it was still quiet. She'd lay out her makeup on the bar, and set about making herself gorgeous.

I had always been obsessed with watching my Mother get ready to go out, watching her put on lipstick and jewellery, and feeling so locked out that because I was a "boy" I wasn't allowed to do this. *(THE PIANIST throws JOHNJOSEPH a headscarf.)* So seeing, for the very first time ever, this hurly burly queen get all glammed up, was more than a revelation. *(JOHNJOSEPH picks a pair of sunglasses out of the onstage detritus.)* As she powdered and shaded her face, and drew on her eyebrows with just two fluid sweeps of her cocoa eyeliner, she educated me.

She schooled me on Andy Warhol and the Stonewall riots, and all those canonical chunks of twentieth century queer history. She told me about new shows on Channel 4, and taught me a lot of very ribald jokes, told me who to watch, and who to watch out for. Then when she was ready, when it was late enough and the bar was full, she would go off to the booth and she'd start to play. It was the same old rubbish she'd played for 20 years but people really got into it. She would always play a Madonna record and dedicate it to me with a wave, so I knew she was watching over me.

THE PIANIST repeats the closing refrain from 'Man of 1000 Faces'.

JOHNJOSEPH: Then I would go out into the crowd and get lost among those sweaty bodies. It was amazing to be fee of my home

life and responsibilities. It liberating, it *was* an education, and I really do miss her.

THE ANIMA appears in wardrobe, as she speaks
JOHNJOSEPH starts to write again.

THE ANIMA: It was my intelligence that set me apart, it was my red hair that set me apart, it was my androgyny that set me apart, it was my archaic way of speaking that set me apart, it was my Mummy's boy persona and my complete distrust for men that set me apart, it was my mortified prudery and my voracious sexual perversions that set me apart. Through all of these things I developed a distance that I could not break, I became less human, I became more object. A pictorial depiction of Odysseus' travels on painted pottery from 600 B.C.E, a relic from antiquity not to be touched.

THE ANIMA goes back in wardrobe.

JOHNJOSEPH: In my late teens, this ability to separate myself from myself made me a perfect, patient fit for fashion photographers for whom I sat mournfully and endlessly, being documented as though for medical records.

THE PIANIST presses play on tape recorder, 'The Model' plays. The wardrobe door opens to reveal THE ANIMA backlit behind a screen.

JOHNJOSEPH and THE PIANIST lip-synch a short extract from 'The Model' and walk as in a runway show. THE ANIMA is seen behind them as a shadow striking elaborate attitudes. After the lip-synch, THE PIANIST returns to the piano, and JOHNJOSEPH freezes in an exaggerated fashion pose. THE ANIMA breaks through the screen, rushing onstage in the manner of a theatre

*dresser. **JOHNJOSEPH** talks aloud whilst she dresses and undresses them.*

JOHNJOSEPH: Modelling was just like my annual childhood visits to the hospital, when I would have to walk up and down the ward, every February, so that the Doctors might figure out why I walked like that. I walked up and down the ward pointlessly, endlessly, as though I were in a runway show. Yes when I walked down the catwalk, at age twenty-three, I could not help but think of those days of being paraded before the doctors at the Alder Hay Children's Hospital. How I would walk down the ward, strike a pose in front of the camera and return back down the catwalk. Yes, and when I went to see casting agents and they barked "Profile, other profile, agency!" it sounded just like my physician's tedious, disinterested demands. It felt just

like sitting secluded in the park at age 14
with my best friend and a strange, unknown
older man, who asked me to roll back my
foreskin for him. Like he was my Doctor, like
he was my agent, like he was a photographer
directing me in front of a camera.

THE ANIMA suddenly strikes the pose
JOHNJOSEPH has been holding, whilst they
break free and circle her.

JOHNJOSEPH: *(To THE ANIMA.)* "Eyes!
Eyes! I need eyes! Stronger eyes! And give
me brow!" Cameras do something to you,
yes, they gorgonise you, they turn you
to stone. That 'click' is the line between
animate life and inanimate death. Cameras
do something to you, yes, gorgonise you,
they make a gorgon of you, something no
one can tear their eyes from, regardless of the
cost. Something, some thing that people will

go to the end of the Earth to seek out, and destroy. *(**THE ANIMA** breaks out of her pose, disconcerted.)*

I was an object d'art from childhood, I was never a person I don't think, I was always a deformed, androgynous, beautiful, silver soup spoon. And there was always someone trying to melt me down for my metal.

*In anger, **THE ANIMA** vandalises the set, spraying a long stripe of blue spray paint over the wardrobe, and piano, then exits through the wardrobe loudly.*

JOHNJOSEPH: I came to New York to do something, I wanted to be something, I wanted to create, I wanted to perform, I wanted to write, so I did. Yes, I did! I got a job compiling the horoscopes for "Go! Magazine", America's most widely distributed

lesbian publication, thank you very much.
Now, I know nothing about astrology,
so I just made it up. It was six months of
"Gemini, this is your lucky month," – I'm a
Gemini so it was always my lucky month –
"Your ship has come in and you have a really
great hairdo."

I literally made it up every month, I think
I jinxed myself a little actually, but what do
I know? The only stars I cared about where
the downtown icons I'd see at parties; Penny
Arcade, Taylor Mac, Justin Bond, who
through several strokes of luck and some
creative accounting with the truth I started
performing with.

*THE PIANIST presses play on his tape deck and
a snatch of 'Teacher's Pet' is heard. THE ANIMA
enters as a schoolboy stripper, coming out of the*

wardrobe she clears discarded costumes, exits
extravagantly.

JOHNJOSEPH: No one I knew in New York
ever had any money, they were all hustlers,
strippers and half-starved writers, no one I
knew ever had a job. Everybody was very
busy of course but nobody had a job. Yet
the booze, the amphetamines, and the
prescription medications were never in short
supply. Whole chunks of my time in New
York are represented to me now as strange
syrupy dreams, with large gaps, sunlight,
twilight pouring in. Once I got so high at a
party that I found myself scrabbling around
the floor of a hotel bathroom in Times Square
looking for a false eyelash which had come
loose. And I was *so* high that I convinced
myself a cockroach had stolen my eyelashes.
I found myself screaming into a crack in

the tile work, "Give me back my eyelashes!
I know you have my eyelashes, you thieving
transvestite cockroach!" The next morning,
I woke up and found those eyelashes on the
bottom of my shoe. Didn't I feel silly?

> *THE ANIMA re-enters through the wardrobe
> dressed in the mismatched skirt and t-shirt outfit
> we have previously seen JOHNJOSEPH wearing.
> It is the end of a long night, she is staring at the
> lights, dragging two tattered feather boas about,
> one shoe in her hand.*

JOHNJOSEPH: The hostel Gina and I were
running soon proved too much like hard
work. We were fundamentally using it to
launch an assault on Manhattan nightlife,
which did not mesh well with our alleged
responsibilities. Nobody in their mid-twenties
should be left in charge of 20 foreign tourists,
especially not two drug addled, glitter covered

drama queens with no experience but sizeable personality disorders. I mean, it was a disaster waiting to happen. And happen it did. It wasn't at all unusual for new guests to arrival at the hostel and find Gina and myself, dressed as Joan and Christina Crawford, squabbling in a sea of Bud Lite cans, with the theme tune to "The Golden Girls" on repeat in the background. Do I even need to tell you that we were promptly fired?

THE PIANIST starts to play 'New York I Love You'.

JOHNJOSEPH: Homeless, helpless and hopeless once more, flat out of luck, flat out of money, and coming down hard on the couch of any friend who would take us in for the night.

JOHNJOSEPH regards THE ANIMA who is sitting on the wardrobe steps looking very

high, they join her. Two verses into the song
THE ANIMA *begins to sing 'I Happen To Like*
New York', and the two songs become a medley.

JOHNJOSEPH: *(Springing up as the song ends.)*
If we're going to be Sartrian about it, and
frankly, why not, that was my fatal instant.
I realised I was right there at the centre of
everything and I had nothing. *(Snatching
up a paper plane from the ground.)* There was
nothing for it but to live. *(He throws the plane
to* **THE ANIMA***. She throws it playfully to* **THE
PIANIST***.)*

JOHNJOSEPH: New York is like that, it is
like an acid bath that strips away the debris,
and leaves you gleaming like a new penny,
like you're perpetually coming up on acid and
thinking, "Oh that's who I am."

THE PIANIST plays a vamp from 'The Apple Stretching'. JOHNJOSEPH exits behind the wardrobe. THE ANIMA opens the wardrobe and grabs handfuls of airplanes from inside. She plays with them, throwing them into the audience and on to the stage, then exits through the wardrobe again. As she does this, JOHNJOSEPH reappears in a dress made entirely of paper planes.

JOHNJOSEPH: *(Finding a pair of earrings onstage and putting them on.)* One sticky spring Manhattan afternoon, I was taking the subway from Washington Heights to Chelsea with my friend Adrian. We had chosen a quiet carriage where we could sit together and discuss matters of importance, when these kids came over and started to make trouble. I don't know why, maybe they didn't like my hairdo, maybe they didn't like my outfit, but they wanted to make trouble. One of them said; "Why the fuck are you wearing that?

Why are you wearing flower pants and a fucking bowtie?"

"It's my sartorial interpretation of Summer," I replied. "Only it's not a bowtie it's a cravat."

"It's a bowtie!"

"No, honestly, it's a cravat," I replied.

This went on for a while until, mercifully my honourable debating partners alighted at Canal St, and I sighed a not so small sigh of relief. I turned to my friend Adrian, who had remained silent throughout the conversation, and said; "Phew! Well, that was close, eh. We could have really found ourselves in trouble there, we got off with just few cross words, they didn't even stab us once!"

And he had the nerve to say to me:

THE PIANIST: *(In an American accent.)* "You need to learn that this is New York, that you can't just go around wearing stuff like that and get away with it."

JOHNJOSEPH: "No," I said, "You need to learn that I can. Do you think that it was iphone wielding, all-in-black, blending-in faggots, that gave you the rights and responsibilities you have today? No! It was frilly, limp wristed kooks, people like Quentin Crisp and Sylvester and Del Martin. People who did not back down on the subway.

THE PIANIST plays 'Call me Drag Queen'.

JOHNJOSEPH picks up a microphone to sing.
THE ANIMA enters with arms full of costume,
throughout the number she gets herself into drag.

JOHNJOSEPH: There I was, propping up the bar of the historic Stonewall Inn,

61

keeping some fabulous company it must be said; Ms. Jonny Woo on one side, Ms. Ana Matronic on the other. The three of us stood there looking like the Witches of Eastwick, when in came a square looking fellow in a suit, made a bee-line for us.

Straight off the cuff he said to me; "I think you're very attractive, is this reciprocated?"

Unimpressed by this less than giving compliment, I told him; "Oh, I'm sorry, I'm married."

"Married?" he asked. "So, like, do you have breasts."

Naturally, I was a little baffled by this complete non sequitur, so I just shook my head.

"No breasts. Oh. Then can I tell you that you're the closest thing to a guy that has ever

made me hard? I mean, you are a guy, right?
I mean, you kinda look like one."

"Oh thank you," I said, "Give me five
minutes to scribble that down in my traveling
dictionary of back-handed compliments."

'Call Me Drag Queen' (reprise).

JOHNJOSEPH: It's not that I don't appreciate
the compliment, I really do appreciate
compliments, please, give me your
compliments. This is a dangerous world and
there are a lot of small minded people out
there, so a creature as glamorous as myself
can't help but feel just a little relieved,
thankful even when the attention is positive.
Complicated genders, complicated bodies
are difficult to, erm grasp, the image of a boy
in a dress is a complicated one to process.
have always said that tranny fuckers are right

there on the vanguard of social and sexual inclusion. *(To **THE PIANIST**.)* I have always said that, haven't I?

THE PIANIST: You have always said that.

'Call Me Drag Queen' (reprise).

JOHNJOSEPH: So I stepped outside to cadge a cigarette out there in the street when this little lady squared up to me and said; "So, you're a drag queen, right?"

"Well, actually it's a bit more complicated than that for me. You see I think of myself as third gendered, transdrogynous."

"Well, you certainly look like a drag queen," she said.

Now, before I could even pull a witty one-liner from my purse, her husband appeared

on the spot to give his feelings on whether or not I was in fact a drag queen. His contribution to the great debate was; "I'm not but if I was, I would."

"Oh really?" I asked, "What is it you're not, and please do tell me what it is you would do if in fact you were."

"I'm not gay," he said, "But if I was I would fancy you."

"Oh, how funny," I replied, "Because I myself am not a pyromaniac, but if I was, I would set you on fire."

Without missing a beat, his wife rejoined the conversation, and said: "And you tell jokes like a drag queen too!"

At that point I gave up and I said, "You're right, you're absolutely right, I am a drag queen. Here

I am squabbling with you over silly sub-genres,
I am a drag queen. It's just as the existentialists
had it; existence precedes essence."

She looked at my blankly, mildly bewildered
and I could tell that she'd had maybe one too
many Bacardi and cokes, and that perhaps she
wasn't as invested in the work of Simone de
Beauvoir as I myself am. I said, "Let me put
it for you like this, in the words of another
great thinker, RuPaul, who wrote, 'We're born
naked, after that it's all drag.'"

I said, "You could say we all create ourselves,
I suppose you could say we're all drag
queens." She liked that, it made her smile.
Then she tripped over a bin bag and fell in a
puddle and it was all kind of embarrassing.

'Call Me Drag Queen' (reprise).

THE ANIMA joins JOHNJOSEPH for a brief vaudeville routine to close the song. At the crescendo THE ANIMA opens an umbrella of glitter over JOHNJOSEPH and exits again through the wardrobe.

JOHNJOSEPH: As a teenage delinquent, in Liverpool, after a night at the Curzon, it was always my plan to take the first train, from Moorfields to Bootle Balliol Road. To head home, to sneak in through the back door before the kids woke up and I was needed for babysitting. That's the only reason anyone would notice I was gone. *(JOHNJOSEPH moves to the wardrobe and picks up the fur coat.)* However, on this particular Sunday, who should I find on the doorstep, but my Mother? *(JOHNJOSEPH sits in front of the wardrobe.)* She'd been out all night and lost her keys, she looked a little panicked,

67

obviously she wanted to be back in the house before my stepfather realised she'd been gone.

My Mother is a very good-looking woman, obviously. She didn't attract her multitudinous husbands with her songbird voice or her encyclopedic knowledge of 19th Century French watercolours, no. She's rather beautiful and very charismatic and people are attracted to her, it's very empowering. For her.

THE PIANIST plays the opening of 'Playboy Mommy'.

JOHNJOSEPH: I was aware, as far back as I can remember, of my Mother having sex, very loudly, with her husbands, with her boyfriends, and other people's husbands and boyfriends, and once I think, with the woman next door who later checked herself into a psychiatric

ward. That is the power of my Mother's sexuality: it literally drives people insane.

Growing up so very Catholic was not conducive to my celebrating my Mother's sexual liberation or the pleasure she took in carnal pursuits. I was a member of the Catholic Young Person's Anti-Abortion League, I was not sexually liberated, I was not enlightened to gender politics or women's rights. So, I found it terribly embarrassing that my Mother ran around town with men she picked up through lonely-hearts columns, and ashamed that everybody knew it.

JOHNJOSEPH sings *'Playboy Mommy'*.

JOHNJOSEPH: Well, why shouldn't my Mother have her very own Summer of Love, every weekend, if she so chose? Why shouldn't she have lovers and toy boys and affairs of the

heart? I was just like every other bastard, just like every other male chauvinist pig. I was obviously just upholding double standards, not just between men and women, but double standards for women on one hand, and my own Mother on the other. And wasn't I going out all night, shagging in public bathrooms, and in Church? I was staying out drinking all night, I was coming home at 6am after pressing myself up against sweaty strangers in a club, and yet I chose to think of myself as just a good time party girl. What a fucking hypocrite! I was ashamed of my Mother, and I was ashamed of being ashamed.

JOHNJOSEPH starts to travel up the ladder to the top of the wardrobe.

JOHNJOSEPH: Sitting on the doorstep that morning, she looked pretty rough, tired, her mascara was smudged, her hair was a mess.

I'm sure I didn't look so hot myself, but I had the backdoor key. We snuck in together, without actually saying anything, we didn't even ask each other where we'd been all night, we just tiptoed into the kitchen and took off our shoes. I went towards the living room, to fake it like I'd passed out in front of the TV and slept there all night. She caught me by the hand and mouthed quietly, "Thank you." I think she meant more than "Thank you for letting me in." She meant, "Thank you for not telling on me. Thank you for not judging me, thank you for not leaving me." And in that quiet moment in the hallway my whole relationship with my Mother was re-contextualised.

JOHNJOSEPH opens the wardrobe to reveal THE ANIMA as Our Lady of The Sacred Heart reworked in drag.

'Playboy Mommy' (reprise).

*As the song ends **JOHNJOSEPH** descends, reaches out to Our Lady and takes the sacred heart from her hand. Inside there is a ring. They take it and put it on, then closes the wardrobe door respectfully.*

JOHNJOSEPH: However there is only so far you can push your luck, and my capacity for luck pushing is practically Sisyphian. I am like Sisyphus with the rock that is my luck pushing it almost, almost to the top of the hill before it comes crashing back down and I have to start all over again.

With the sand under my feet slowly falling away, with the ocean coming in stealthily, I stood on the beach at Coney Island, contemplating time. For the first time I had found home, I had seen it for myself

I had touched it. It was New York in all
of her cracked out, hyperbolic, fraudulent
grandiosity. She had taken me to her bosom
and nourished me, to lose her was almost
more than I could bear.

It was the middle of Summer and it had
recently became official that I was being swept
back out to sea. My totally illegal, somewhat
immoral presence in America had come to the
attention of the powers that be. And nothing
could convince them that I was anything but
a blood sucking illegal immigrant.

*THE PIANIST interrupts by pushing the tape
recorder button again. The 'Benny Hill' theme
blares out. THE ANIMA appears wearing a
ridiculous combination of all of her costumes.
She proceeds to strip them off, at first eager to
please, gradually becoming tired, then frustrated.
Finally she is left in just her white underwear,*

identical to the pair we have seen JOHNJOSEPH
wear during their onstage strips and changes.
THE PIANIST stops the tape, THE ANIMA
freezes, and JOHNJOSEPH begins to speak.

JOHNJOSEPH: I suppose I did it. I must
have allowed myself to be made an object of,
I must have enjoyed it or else I would not
have been so passive in my transformation. It
didn't matter to me if people were yelling:

THE PIANIST: I love you!

JOHNJOSEPH: Or simply

THE PIANIST: Shut the door!

JOHNJOSEPH: Because it was all white noise,
a sculptural, sepulchral white noise which had
dislocated me from and chance of subjectivity.
Try as you may, you can't execute a soup
spoon, no, you can't humiliate a soup spoon.

All I had to do was leave my personhood behind on the shore and step into the boat.

I stood facing the Atlantic, it was the day of the famous Mermaid Parade with all of my friends crammed on the boardwalk in their finery, yelling in the midday sun. Gina was smoking a cigarette, we watched beautiful boys burst out of the ocean and run glistening back to their families. I turned to her and said, "If I had been born a real girl, things would have been so much easier."

Gina said, "Yeah JJ, a vagina, and your life would be perfect."

My love affair had not been a monogamous marriage, it was an illicit, behind closed doors charade, we knew we would be found out but that didn't mean it wouldn't hurt. Standing there facing the Atlantic, like Canute on

the shore in a floral print swimsuit, I could not hold back the tide, I felt the end arrive. I acquiesced to the waves. Hello Charon.

THE ANIMA presses tape recorder and a burst of 'Get Happy' plays. JOHNJOSEPH lip-synchs to the track as THE PIANIST begins to play 'Pissing in a River'. JOHNJOSEPH begins singing 'Pissing in a River' and kicks out a roll of plastic sheeting in front of them, as they walk the stage mournfully. THE ANIMA approaches JOHNJOSEPH with a bucket full of blue paint and brushes. She applies the paint to JOHNJOSEPH as they sing, as though she were painting her portrait on their body, as though she were an artist bringing her canvas to life. As the song ends, THE ANIMA exits through the wardrobe. JOHNJOSEPH, exhausted and alone, tears the paint covered paper dress from their body and stands in their white underwear, red socks and gold shoes, splattered in paint, encrusted in glitter. THE PIANIST strikes the

same repetitive high note we have heard earlier,
in the public toilet scene.

JOHNJOSEPH: I remember being ten and
waking up in the middle of the night because
my Mother was sobbing. I went downstairs
and found that her husband had her pinned
against the wall, with a hammer raised above
her head, ready to strike. I ran for help, I
woke the neighbours up and we got back,
just in time to see him take that hammer and
smash everything in our pathetic little council
house to pieces. The doors, the windows, the
furniture, the fish bowl, mirrors, the TV, the
light fixtures, electrical appliances, the sink.

Everything was completely demolished,
shattered, destroyed. The carpet was full of
thousands of pieces of glass, it looked like an
earthquake had hit us, just us, and moved on,
and when they finally pulled my step-father

out of the house there wasn't a plate or a bowl left whole.

The entire place was glinting with reflected light, gleaming with buried shards of glass, shining with the mysterious illumination of a Cathedral. Horrible, beautiful, and silent. A neighbour took out the hoover and started cleaning up the mess. She said, "You're gonna be finding bits of glass in your carpets for months 'ere." *(**JOHNJOSEPH** scoops to pick up glitter tape from the earlier umbrella glitter drop.)* And we did.

But now that image, more than any other, that image best defines my childhood and all of its strange magic, violence, poverty, sexuality, loss, terror, and black humour. You see, you can have nothing, and you can have that nothing taken from you, and you can still go on. You can live in the debris and you

can live to tell the tale. You can pick up those fragments and make yourself a crown.

JOHNJOSEPH sprinkles a handful of the glitter tape over their head. They holds their arms out wide, as the lights fade to black. THE PIANIST strikes one final chord.

Fin